CW00494301

Tiffintastic

Laura Kirkman

A Quick Brown Fox Publications Book

First published in Great Britain by Quick Brown Fox Publications in 2012

Copyright © Laura Kirkman 2012

The moral right of the author has been asserted

All rights reserved. No part of this publication may be reproduced, stored in a retrieval system,
or transmitted in any form or by any means, without the prior permission in writing of the publisher,
nor be otherwise circulated in any form of binding or cover other than that in which it is published
and without a similar condition including this condition being imposed on the subsequent purchaser.

ISBN 9780956407924

Cover design © Adam Kirkman 2012, images © Laura Kirkman

Images on pp4, 6, 8, 11, 15, 19, 23, 25, 27, 31, 33, 35, 39, 41, 43, 47, 49, 51, 52-3, 54 © Laura Kirkman 2012
Images on pp12, 14, 16, 20-21, 28-29, 36-37, 44-45 © istockphoto.com

Photography by Mark Bastick, www.markbastick.co.uk

www.quickbrownfoxpublications.co.uk

TIFFINTASTIC

LAURA KIRKMAN

To E Lizabeth
Happy eating
Laura

QUICK BROWN FOX PUBLICATIONS

Kirkman
2012 xxx.

Contents

Spring
Almond Liqueur Tiffin
Fudge Tiffin
Easter Tiffin

Summer
White Chocolate and Ginger Tiffin
Summer Lemon Tiffin
Irish Cream Liqueur Tiffin

Autumn
Earl Grey Tiffin
Cherry and Kirsch Tiffin
Coffee and Walnut Tiffin

Winter
Coconut Tiffin
Rock Tiffin
Christmas Tiffin

What is tiffin?

Tiffin is a decadently delicious mix of chocolate, biscuit and fruit – a multi-layered sensation that tantalises the tastebuds. The smooth velvety chocolate taste comes first before the biscuity crunch heralds the arrival of the fruit flavours bursting onto your palate. Finally, the alcohol gives a well-rounded finish which leaves your mouth watering for more. Quite simply, the taste of heaven on a plate!

Originally, tiffin was the name of a light midday meal and was used as the local name for afternoon tea in British Colonial India. The British then adopted the name itself to mean afternoon tea, from a now disused slang word *tiffining*, meaning 'taking a little drink or sip' – tiff, in this case, meaning sip. For the British, 'time for tiffin' then came to mean 'time for afternoon tea' – and who doesn't like a sweet something with their afternoon tea?

Later, the word tiffin became synonymous with this sweet something, which eventually evolved into our modern concept of tiffin, now made with a variety of fruits, crushed biscuits and chocolate. Tiffin also goes under the ungainly American name of refrigerator cake, so-called because the tiffin-creating process involves no baking.

How to make tiffin

Tiffin has four simple components:

- A rich, chocolatey sauce – to bind the ingredients together
- Biscuits – to supply the splendidly satisfying crunch component
- Dried fruit and nuts – whatever you fancy, or is available in the cupboard and can be combined to create a distinctive tiffin. Liquor and spirits add a luxurious dimension to the tiffin but can be added or left out according to your taste preferences
- Toppings – not just a lavish smothering of yet more chocolate, but rather a show for the eyes which ensures the tiffin is as good to your eyes as it is on your tastebuds

The wonderful thing about tiffin is that if you keep the four components in mind (and, crucially, their appropriate ratios) then you can create your own unending variety of uniquely designed tiffin.

On the following pages are some helpful hints on selecting suitable ingredients for the recipes in this book. You can also use these to add to your own tiffin creations!

Chocolate: the do's and the don'ts

Do use a high quality chocolate with a high cocoa content, this makes it suitable for cooking. A good quality chocolate produces a much smoother result.

Do melt the chocolate in a bowl suspended over a pan of gently simmering water as this ensures the slow melting of the chocolate.

Don't let the bowl touch the water or the chocolate could overheat.

Don't allow any water to come into contact with the chocolate as that will cause the chocolate to seize and become lumpy and grainy, before stiffening and then becoming unworkable. Chocolates seizes because the dry cocoa and sugar particles become moist and stick together.

Don't panic if the chocolate seizes! To rescue seized chocolate, immediately remove the chocolate from the heat. Gradually add one or two teaspoons of vegetable oil, stirring all the time, until the chocolate becomes smooth again.

Don't panic if the chocolate overheats, either! Immediately remove it from the heat and transfer it to a cool, dry bowl. Add a handful of solid chocolate pieces to further cool the mixture down, stirring continuously until melted. If it remains lumpy, stir through a sieve then treat as if it had seized, as above.

Do take special care with white chocolate. Its cocoa butter has a lower melting point than darker chocolate and a narrow range between this and its burning point. Stir regularly to ensure an even spread of heat and watch carefully - white chocolate seems to have the ability to be solid one moment, then lumpy and burnt the next…

Don't be afraid to use the microwave! Although it is easy to burn in the microwave, you can avoid that by using short, sharp bursts of 10-15 seconds, stirring in between. When just a few lumps remain, it is sufficiently melted - these will melt when you stir the chocolate.

The additives

There is nothing quite as frustrating in life as looking at a long list of ingredients and knowing that you do not have them in your store cupboard - or, worse, believing that they are there, until opening the cupboard reveals otherwise! Well, do not despair - rather, get sassy with your cupboard and substitute using what you have.

You can try alternative fruits such as dates, raisins, sultanas, currants, dried figs and cherries; or alternative nuts like pecans, walnuts, hazelnuts - or leave them out entirely if you're not a nut lover (or they don't love you). Sweets add another character element - if you think it should work, why not give it a try?

Alcohol: the soaking

For a real depth of flavour you can leave the dried fruits and other ingredients soaking overnight in alcohol to absorb the flavours. (For a less intense flavour, just soak for 30 minutes while you prepare the tiffin.) The majority use alcohol, but don't feel like you have to! Remember: experimentation is the key to choosing which spirit will enhance the ingredients. Spirits like rum, brandy and whisky work well, as do fortified wines like port and sherry. Liqueurs and chocolate are a marriage made in heaven but if you wish a non-alcoholic alternative, why not try tea or coffee?

Biscuits

As in life, so with tiffin: you can have endless debates about the various merits of different biscuits. For tiffin, though, the crunch factor is all-important. Plain biscuits work well as they retain their crunch and 'also balance out the richness of the chocolate. Some biscuits absorb more of the melted chocolate than others; you may therefore need to adjust the ratio of biscuit to chocolate to bind the tiffin together successfully. A Rich Tea, for example, seems to require a reduction whereas, say, a bourbon does not.

Another key factor is the size of the crushed biscuit and the method of crushing it. You need fairly evenly-sized chunks to keep the tiffin together, so chunks around 1-1.5 centimetres are preferable. Cheesecake base consistency is too fine; this will just absorb the chocolate.

The crushing method is up to you, I prefer to place my biscuits in a freezer bag and take out any pent-up aggression on them using the end of a rolling pin handle! Shortbread fingers and bourbons require a much more controlled approach and should either be cut into equal sizes with a sharp knife or, if you like the more rustic approach, broken up by hand.

How many portions?

Well, that depends on you. These recipe quantities make 20-25 generously sized squares, but can be adapted to be more generous (or less generous!) depending on your mood, budget, size of tin, or even just how much you like your guests! As for calories - you just have to accept that there are many, and enjoy the moment.

Storage

Tiffin can be stored in the fridge for up to a week. Tiffin also freezes well so any excess can be saved for another occasion, unexpected guests or other emergency tiffin requirements.

Equipment

- Baking tin - all recipes use a 20x26cm (8x10") shallow baking tin, unless otherwise stated
- Greaseproof paper - to line the tin, leave the ends long to aid lifting the tiffin out
- Saucepan - to simmer the water in
- Small heat-proof bowl - sized to fit the saucepan rim but suspended clear of the gently simmering water
- Large bowl - to soak the fruits in, and for mixing the tiffin
- Rolling pin - to bash the biscuits
- Large freezer bag - to place the biscuits in to be bashed
- Measuring scales - goes without saying!
- Mixing spoon - to mix it all together
- Plastic or silicon spatula - to ensure all the ingreditents get into the tin
- Metal spoon - to press down the tiffin to ensure it sets together
- Palette knife - to smooth the melted chocolate on top
- Large sharp knife - to cut the tiffin into the desired size
- Large chopping board - large enough to cut the whole tiffin on
- Zester or small grater - to remove the outer layer of citrus fruit for flavouring

SPRING

Almond Liqueur Tiffin

This tiffin was created to celebrate a recent birthday of mine and contains many of my favourite ingredients - so, to me, it is a small slice of what heaven may taste like. This is divine as petit fours with a glass of Amaretto. For added elegance, place whole Amaretti biscuits in the bottom of the tin to mark out portion sizes: careful though, if you use mini Amaretti, they may float away!

Shopping List

600g dark chocolate

250g Amaretti biscuits

230g butter

100g dried apricots

100g whole almonds

4 tbs golden syrup

4 tbs almond liqueur

Makes 20-25 portions

To soak
100g whole almonds
100g dried apricots
4 tbs almond liqueur

To melt
400g dark chocolate
200g butter
4 tbs golden syrup

To add
250g Amaretti biscuits

To top with
200g dark chocolate
30g butter

Roughly chop the almonds (skin on) and apricots, place in a large bowl and cover with the four tablespoons of almond liqueur. This stage is best started the night before to allow time for the flavours to develop (eight to ten hours).

Grease and line a 20x26cm (8x10") baking tin. Place the whole Amaretti biscuits to line the bottom and gently crush the remaining biscuits in a freezer bag and reserve for later.

Melt the chocolate, butter and golden syrup in a bowl suspended over a pan of gently simmering water, stirring occasionally until all combined and completely melted. Pour this over the almond mixture.

Add the crushed biscuits and mix until well coated. Pour over the whole biscuits in the tin and then press down with the back of a metal spoon to level before placing in the fridge to set while you prepare the topping.

Melt the remaining dark chocolate and butter and then pour over the top of the tiffin, smoothing the surface with a palette knife - it is normal to have both fruits and nuts poking out of the topping. Leave overnight in the fridge to set before cutting into squares. Remember, care is needed when cutting to include a whole Amaretti biscuit in the squares as the biscuits are brittle when cut.

Fudge Tiffin

This tiffin was created one sunny, summer's afternoon by a psychology student and a midwife. The ready-made fudge sauce was an inspired choice for a lighter summer tiffin and the whisky can be used to complement the fudge sauce for a grown-up version, but it does work just as well without the whisky.

Shopping List
300g white chocolate
250g Rich Tea biscuits
100g butter
150g fudge sauce
100g sultanas
75g raisins
3 tbs golden syrup
2 tbs whisky
Makes 20-25 portions

To soak
2 tbs whisky
(optional, for the fruit)

To melt
300g white chocolate
100g butter
3 tbs golden syrup

To add
250g Rich Tea biscuits
150mls ready-made fudge sauce
100g sultanas
75g raisins

To top with
Nothing - it's beautiful as it is!

Grease and line a 20x8cm (8x3") loaf tin, leaving plenty of paper at the ends to press down the tiffin to compact later.

Add the sultanas and raisins to a large bowl. (If using whisky, this is best started the night before - pour two tablespoons of whisky over the fruit and leave to soak.) Roughly break up the Rich Tea biscuits and place with the dried fruit.

Melt the chocolate, butter and golden syrup in a bowl suspended over a pan of gently simmering water until completely melted, stirring occasionally until all combined and pour over the other ingredients.

Add the fudge sauce and stir well until all the ingredients are combined and coated in the chocolatey mixture.

Transfer to the loaf tin and ensure all ingredients are firmly compacted by covering and pressing with the extra greaseproof paper ends. Finally, place in the fridge to set.

Easter Tiffin

Just think of the tastes of Easter – combine them into one tiffin and this is what you get! Easter biscuits meet Easter eggs and marzipan, a divine way to mark the end of Lent. You can decorate with Easter eggs and chicks if you so desire, and if you can't find Easter biscuits, currant biscuits will do!

Shopping List
600g white chocolate
250g Easter biscuits
200g mini Easter eggs
200g marzipan
150g butter
30g currants
20g sultanas
20g candied peel
4 tbs golden syrup
Fluffy chick or two
Makes 20-25 portions

To soak
There's nothing to soak, so you can make this one straight away!

To melt
400g white chocolate
125g butter
4 tbs golden syrup

To add
250g Easter biscuits
200g marzipan
100g mini-eggs
30g currants
20g candied peel
20g sultanas

To top with
200g white chocolate
100g mini-eggs
25g butter

Grease and line the tin: 20x26cm (8x10") should suffice for a deep tiffin.

Break up the biscuits into 1-1.5cm chunks and place in large bowl along with candied peel, currants, sultanas, mini Easter eggs and marzipan cut into ½ cm pieces.

Melt the chocolate and butter in a bowl suspended over a pan of gently simmering water until completely melted, stirring occasionally until all combined. Pour the melted chocolate over the biscuit mixture and add the golden syrup before mixing well. Transfer the tiffin mixture to the tin, pushing down well to level the surface, and place in the fridge to set.

For the topping, melt the remaining white chocolate and butter, stirring regularly to ensure that it doesn't burn. Pour the melted chocolate over the tiffin and smooth over with a palette knife.

Place 20-25 mini-eggs at regular intervals to mark out the centre of the Tiffin pieces. Random placement may look attractive at this stage - until you have the challenge of cutting through them before serving.

SUMMER

White Chocolate and Ginger Tiffin

This conjures up memories of a wonderful, warm summer afternoon spent match-making alcohol to biscuits. This combination worked out best by far, although still tastes divine without the wine - so you decide. This tiffin was created for Cara, who was unable to eat cocoa at the time.

Shopping List
400g white chocolate
300g gingernut biscuits
160g crystallised ginger
135g butter
50g sultanas
30g dried dates
3 tbs ginger wine
3 tbs golden syrup
1 tsp ground ginger
Makes 20-25 portions

To soak
100g crystallised ginger
50g sultanas
30g dried dates
3tbs ginger wine (optional)

To add
300g gingernuts
3 tbs golden syrup
1 tsp ground ginger

To melt
200g white chocolate
100g butter

To top with
200g white chocolate
35g butter
60g crystallised ginger

Roughly chop the crystallised stem ginger and place with the sultanas and dates in a large bowl and cover with ginger wine (if using). Crush the gingernuts in a freezer bag using the handle of a rolling pin and set aside for later.

Grease and line the baking tin - a 20x26cm (8x10") works well.

Melt the chocolate and butter in a bowl suspended over a pan of gently simmering water until completely melted, stirring occasionally until all combined. Next, place the biscuit pieces with one teaspoon of ground ginger and three tablespoons of golden syrup into the large bowl with the fruit mixture.

Pour the melted chocolate over the mixture and stir until all ingredients have a good covering of chocolate. Transfer the tiffin mixture to the tin and use the back of a metal spoon to press down the mixture. Place in fridge to set.

Melt the remaining chocolate with the butter in the original chocolate bowl, again over the pan of gently simmering water. Pour the melted chocolate over the tiffin mixture and smooth with a palette knife before finally decorating by gently sprinkling with the remaining finely-chopped crystallised ginger before returning to the fridge.

Summer Lemon Tiffin

Think of a balmy summer's day and resting from the midday sun in the cool of a lemon grove. Imagine sipping a refreshingly cool fruit cocktail on a warm evening. Summer lemon tiffin evokes these holiday memories and provides a lighter alternative for summer. The fresh lemon and alcoholic summer drink cut through an otherwise indulgent and creamy tiffin. The pistachios, cranberries and lemon swirls create a visual feast that really tastes as good as it looks!

Shopping List
500g white chocolate
250g shortbread fingers
75g sultanas
130g butter
70g dried cranberries
60g pistachio nuts
3 tbs golden syrup
3 tbs Limoncello
Small jar lemon curd
Lemon
Makes 20-25 portions

To soak
75g sultanas
50g dried cranberries
40g pistachio nuts
3 tbs Limoncello
Zest of 1 lemon

To melt
300g white chocolate
100g butter

To add
250g shortbread fingers
3 tbs golden syrup

To top with
200g white chocolate
30g butter

For decoration
20g pistachios
20g dried cranberries
2 tbs lemon curd

Grease and line the 20x26cm (8x10") tin. Next, zest the lemon to remove the intense citrus flavour by removing the outer layer of peel and add this to a large bowl with sultanas, cranberries and pistachios, covering with the Limoncello, setting aside for half an hour. Next, cut up the shortbread fingers - each into approximately five 1cm pieces - and place with the golden syrup in the large bowl with the lemon mixture.

After all this is prepared, melt the chocolate and butter in a bowl suspended over a pan of gently simmering water until completely melted, stirring occasionally until all combined.

Add the melted chocolate mixture to the other ingredients in the large bowl and mix well. Transfer the tiffin to the lined tin and press down with the back of a large metal spoon - the tiffin can be quite uneven at this point with large boulders of shortbread popping out, but the topping will balance this out. Place the tiffin in the fridge to set.

Melt the remaining chocolate and butter and then pour over the set tiffin. Smooth the surface with a pallete knife and sprinkle over the remaining cranberries and pistachios. Finally, mix the lemon curd with two tablespoons of boiling water and use a piping bag or spoon to swirl a pattern of your choice onto the topping. Return to the fridge to set overnight before cutting and serving.

Irish Cream Liqueur Tiffin

The ultimate girly tiffin, thought up after a girls' night in - the perfect way to let your hair down with friends! The smooth seduction of the Irish Cream liqueur, mixed with the childhood innocence of milk and cookies, gives rise to a smooth, well-rounded tiffin that slips down delightfully - just like the drink that inspired it!

Shopping List

500g milk chocolate
400g choc chip cookies
125g butter
100g fudge pieces
50g sultanas
50g raisins
50g dried dates
4 tbs Irish Cream liqueur
3 tbs golden syrup

Makes 20-25 portions

To soak
50g sultanas
50g raisins
50g dried dates
4 tbs Irish Cream liqueur

To add
400g chocolate chip cookies

To melt
300g milk chocolate
100g butter
3 tbs golden syrup

To top with
200g milk chocolate
100g fudge pieces
25g butter

Place the sultanas, currants and dates in large bowl and cover with the Irish Cream liqueur and leave to soak for just half an hour while you prepare the rest of the tiffin; any longer and the dates turn into a soggy mush.

Then grease and line a 20x26cm (8x10") baking tin. Crush the chocolate chip cookies in a freezer bag using the handle of a rolling pin and place in the large bowl with the dried fruit mixture of sultanas, raisins and dates.

Melt the chocolate, butter and syrup in a bowl suspended over a pan of gently simmering water until completely melted, stirring occasionally until all combined. Immediately pour the chocolate mixture over the other ingredients in the bowl, stirring until well combined. Transfer the mixture into the lined tin and press down with the back of a metal spoon before placing in the fridge.

Now, cut the fudge pieces into still smaller pieces - roughly half a centimetre square - before preparing the topping. For this, melt the remaining milk chocolate and butter and smooth over the tiffin surface using a palette knife.

Finally, sprinkle the chopped fudge evenly over the topping, returning afterwards to the fridge to set prior to cutting.

Earl Grey Tiffin

Tea drinking is both a national habit and obsession. Girl friends often pop in for a pot of Earl Grey and a natter. What tiffin could be better suited for the occasion than one deeply infused with both the aroma and taste of Earl Grey tea? Fresh lemon zest picks up the subtle infusion of the tea's Bergamot. This tiffin is the perfect companion for a relaxed afternoon tea, whatever the occasion. Loose Earl Grey tea creates a richer flavour, but tea bags are also fine.

Shopping List
400g milk chocolate
250g shortbread
250g milk chocolate
and nougat bar
150g chocolate truffles
100g raisins
80g butter
75g currants
6 tbs Earl Grey tea leaves
3 tbs golden syrup
lemon
Makes 20-25 portions

To soak
100g raisins
75g currants
6 tbs loose Earl Grey tea
Zest of 1 lemon

To add
250g shortbread fingers

To melt
250g milk chocolate nougat bar
200g milk chocolate
50g butter
3 tbs golden syrup

To top with
200g milk chocolate
150g truffles
30g butter

Make up a small amount of strong Earl Grey tea; six tablespoons of loose tea in 150mls of boiling water (or three teabags in 100mls water) creates the ideal strength. Place the raisins, currants and lemon zest in a large bowl and pour the Earl Grey tea over them and leave for 30 minutes to let the flavours fully absorb.

Meanwhile, grease and line a 20x26cm (8x10") baking tin and cut the shortbread into five pieces about one centimetre long. Next melt the chocolate, the milk chocolate and nougat bar, butter and golden syrup in a bowl suspended over a pan of gently simmering water until completely melted, stirring occasionally until all combined.

Quickly drain off any remaining tea from your mixing bowl and combine the shortbread biscuits with the soaked fruits. Pour the melted chocolate mixture over the soaked fruits and stir until combined. Transfer to the tin, smooth down with the back of a metal spoon and place in the fridge.

Melt the remaining chocolate and butter in a bowl suspended over a pan of gently simmering water and then smooth over the chilled tiffin. Roughly chop the truffle pieces before sprinkling over the melted chocolate. Leave in the fridge to set overnight before serving it with – you guessed it - Earl Grey tea!

Cherry and Kirsch Tiffin

Think Black Forest gateau for this dark and fruity tiffin - it's drenched in Kirsch, adding a distinctive edge that cuts through the bitter richness of the chocolate. Just the perfect tiffin to savour after an autumnal country walk under blue skies when curling up in front of a roaring fire with a good book.

Shopping List

500g 70% dark chocolate
300g bourbon biscuits
155g butter
150g dried sour cherries
60g dried figs
50g dried cranberries
8 tbs Kirsch
4 tbs golden syrup
Makes 20-25 portions

To soak
100g dried sour cherries
60g dried figs
50g dried cranberries
6 tbs Kirsch

To melt
300g bitter dark chocolate
125g butter
4 tbs golden syrup

To add
300g bourbon biscuits

To top with
200g dark chocolate
50g dried sour cherries
30g butter
2 tbs Kirsch

This tiffin is best started the night before to allow plenty of time for the fruits to absorb the flavour of the Kirsch. In a large bowl, place the sour cherries, cranberries and roughly-chopped figs, then pour over six tablespoons of Kirsch.

In a separate, smaller bowl, pour two tablespoons of Kirsch over the remaining 50g of sour cherries - this is for the topping. Cover both bowls with a clean tea towel and leave overnight for the flavours to develop.

Grease and line a 20x26cm (8x10") baking tin. Roughly cut the bourbon biscuits into four pieces using a sharp knife. Melt the chocolate, butter and golden syrup in a bowl suspended over a pan of gently simmering water until completely melted, stirring occasionally until all combined.

Next, mix the melted chocolate and biscuit pieces into the soaked fruits and transfer into the greased and lined tin, pressing down with the back of a metal spoon before placing in the fridge to set.

For the topping, melt the remaining chocolate and butter over pan of gently simmering water, spread over tiffin with a palette knife until smooth. Finally, cut the soaked sour cherries into two or three pieces (dependent on size) and sprinkle over the tiffin before returning to the fridge to set overnight.

Coffee and Walnut Tiffin

Coffee and walnut is a bittersweet English afternoon classic. Rum and raisin was another close contender for this afternoon classic, but you can adapt this recipe to create that, too! This one is best started the night before to leave time for the raisins and sultanas to swell and absorb the coffee. For a more intense flavour, leave this to soak in a small box for a few days – giving it the odd shake!

Shopping List
500g dark chocolate
250g Rich Tea biscuits
140g butter
100g walnuts
50g milk chocolate
50g raisins
50g sultanas
3 tbs ground coffee
2 tbs golden syrup
Makes 20-25 portions

To soak
100g walnuts
50g raisins
50g sultanas
3 tbs gound coffee

To melt
300g dark chocolate
100g butter
3 tbs golden syrup

To add
250g Rich Tea biscuits

To top with
200g dark chocolate
50g milk chocolate
40g butter

Start by making a strong coffee using 3 tbs ground coffee to 150mls boiling water, alternatively 2 tbs instant coffee to 100 mls water. Add the raisins, sultanas, walnuts to a box and pour the coffee over them, then seal and leave overnight - or for a couple of days if you have time.

When ready to start making the tiffin, grease and line the 20x26cm (8x10") baking tin. Transfer your soaked fruits to a large, dry bowl. Crush the biscuits into one centimetre sized pieces, by placing them inside a freezer bag and using the handle of the rolling pin, before adding to the soaked fruit.

Now, melt the chocolate, butter and golden syrup in a bowl suspended over a pan of gently simmering water until completely melted, stirring occasionally until all combined. Pour the melted chocolate over the other ingredients, stirring until well combined and transfer to the lined tin, pressing down with the back of a metal spoon, before placing in the fridge to set.

Using the same bowl, melt the dark chocolate with 20g of butter. At the same time, in a separate bowl, melt the white chocolate with the remaining butter. Pour the melted dark chocolate over the the tiffin and smooth with a palette knife; then immediately pour the melted white chocolate on in large blobs and swirl the two together with a cake skewer to create a feathered effect. Return to the fridge to set.

You can make rum and raisin tiffin by substituting three tablespoons of rum for coffee and replacing the dark and milk chocolate with milk and white chocolate respectively, then follow the recipe above.

WINTER

Coconut Tiffin

Also known as 'Seed Tiffin', this was commissioned for Mr and Mrs Seed's wedding - as the happy couple originally met in Bosnia, the special ingredient of Basanski Lokum biscuits (a Bosnian delicacy - chocolate and coconut shortbread biscuit) were shipped in specially for the occasion. Additionally, traditional Bosnian Sljivovica (plum brandy) kept the Bosnian theme - but if you are unable to locate either ingredient, coconut cookies and brandy work well as substitutes.

Shopping List
400g dark chocolate
300g coconut cookies
150g butter
100g dried cranberries
100g glacé cherries
50g dried sour cherries
50g desiccated coconut
50g white chocolate
4 tbs plum brandy
3 tbs golden syrup
Makes 20-25 portions

To soak
100g dried cranberries
100g glacé cherries
50g dried sour cherries
4 tbs plum brandy

To add
300g coconut cookies
50g desiccated coconut

To melt
200g dark chocolate
100g butter
3 tbs golden syrup

To top with
200g dark chocolate
50g white chocolate
50g butter

Place the cranberries, glacé cherries and sour cherries in a large bowl and pour the plum brandy over them. Leave overnight to allow the fruit to swell and absorb the brandy and its flavours.

Grease and line a 20x26cm (8x10") baking tin. Place the biscuits in a freezer bag and crush using the end of a rolling pin and reserve these for later.

Melt the chocolate, butter and golden syrup in a bowl suspended over a pan of gently simmering water until completely melted, stirring occasionally until all combined. Once the chocolate mixture is melted, pour over the soaked fruits, then add the desiccated coconut and crushed biscuits. Stir until all the ingredients are well coated, then transfer to the tin and smooth with the back of a metal spoon before placing in the fridge to set.

Using the same bowl melt the dark chocolate with 25g of the butter until melted. At the same time in a separate bowl melt the white chocolate and remaining butter. Pour the melted dark chocolate all over the tiffin and feather the melted white chocolate onto it. Return to the fridge and allow to set.

Rock Tiffin *An ode to rocky road...*

A tiffin fit for a princess, studded with pink and green jewels. The sourness of the cranberries counterbalances the sweetness of the marshmallow while the crunchiness of the pistachios contrasts with the marshmallow's gooeyness, creating a beautiful tiffin that will surprise and delight a beautiful princess - or prince! You may question the Turkish Delight - but try it and see. You won't be disappointed...

Shopping List
600g milk chocolate
150g Turkish Delight
125g butter
100g marshmallows
50g meringue
50g pistachio nuts
50g cranberries
2 x 40g chocolate-covered honeycomb bars
3 tbs golden syrup
Makes 20-25 portions

To soak
There's nothing to soak for this recipe, so you can get started straight away!

To add
150g Turkish Delight
100g marshmallows
50g meringue
50g pistachio nuts
50g dried cranberries

To melt
400g milk chocolate
100g butter
3 tbs golden syrup

To top with
200g milk chocolate
25g butter
2 x 40g chocolate-covered honeycomb bars

Grease and line a 20x26cm (8x10") baking tin. Then cut up the marshmallows and Turkish Delight into quarters and place in a large bowl with the roughly broken meringues, adding the cranberries and pistachios.

Next, melt the chocolate, butter and golden syrup in a bowl suspended over a pan of gently simmering water until completely melted, stirring occasionally until all combined.

Once melted, pour the chocolate mixture over the other ingredients and stir until they are thoroughly coated. Don't worry at this stage if it looks rather grainy; that's the chocolate melting the meringue and it's delicious. Transfer the tiffin mixture to the tin and smooth with the back of a metal spoon before placing in the fridge to set. Next, using the same bowl, melt the remaining chocolate and butter and pour over the tiffin and smooth with a palette knife.

Break up the honeycomb chocolate bars in their packs by crushing with a rolling pin until you have a fine, rough dust, then sprinkle thickly over the tiffin. Return the tiffin to the fridge and leave overnight to set.

Christmas Tiffin

This is tiffin infused with all the aroma and taste sensations of Christmas: brandy, clementines and spiced biscuits. German spiced biscuits are available from supermarkets at Christmas - the hard Spekulatius biscuits give excellent results. Best started the night before to allow the flavours to absorb.

Shopping List
500g dark chocolate
350g German biscuits
125g butter
60g sultanas
60g currants
60g raisins
50g glacé ginger
4 tbs brandy, or port
3 tbs golden syrup
½ tsp ginger
½ tsp cinnamon
clementine
Makes 20-25 portions

To soak
60g sultanas
60g raisins
60g currants
3 tbs brandy, or port
Zest of 1 clementine

To add
350g German biscuits
½ tsp ginger
½ tsp cinnamon

To melt
300g dark chocolate
100g butter
3 tbs golden syrup

To top with
200g dark chocolate
50g glacé ginger, or cut mixed peel
25g butter

Start by placing the sultanas, raisins, currants and zest of one clementine into a large bowl and pour over the port or brandy, cover with a clean tea towel and leave overnight. You can, of course, replace the port or brandy with any spirit that represents Christmas to you.

Grease and line a tin – a 20x26cm (8x10") baking tin works well. Place the spiced Spekulatius biscuits into a freezer bag and crush them into half to one centimetre sized pieces before adding them into the large bowl with the soaked fruit mixture.

Melt the chocolate, butter and golden syrup in a bowl suspended over a pan of gently simmering water until completely melted, stirring occasionally until all combined.

Transfer the melted chocolate to the large bowl with the dried fruits and biscuits. Stir all of the ingredients together to ensure everything gets a thorough chocolate coating. Transfer the tiffin mixture to the tin and smooth with the back of a metal spoon before placing in the fridge to set.

For the topping, melt the remaining chocolate and butter in the same bowl over a pan of gently simmering water. Pour this over the tiffin and smooth the surface with a palette knife before sprinkling the finely-chopped glacé ginger (or cut mixed peel) over the top. Return the tiffin to the fridge to set.

Acknowledgements

My thanks go out to the many people who have made *Tiffintastic* possible. A work made in love that has been many years in labour. Special thanks to PSJ for the orginal 'tiffin mania' and all that followed.

Tiffintastic would not have come about without the numerous people who have helped at each stage along the way. People I wish to specifically acknowledge for making this possible are as follows: special thanks to Adam for his time, energy and enthusiasm for making this project come to book. (Adam, in turn, would like to thank the long-suffering Liz and the marvellous Marina.) To my parents, Keith and Jancy, for allowing the photoshoot to slowly take over their house - who would have thought our biggest problem in October would be the unseasonal heat wave melting all the chocolate? Special thanks to Jancy for her work on the text, and to Granny for her collection of teacups and saucers. To Mark Bastick for venturing into food photography and helping make chocolate look attractive in a kind of 'I want to eat this' way (check out his website at www.markbastick.co.uk).

To Liz, Fiona and Katie for their overwhelming enthusiasm. To Becca for our great 'tiffintat' outing. Kate M for her artistic endeavours. Catherine for help with the props and the many others there isn't space to mention, but you know who you are.

To the many midwives and other maternity staff who have eaten their way through a goodly amount of tiffin as the recipes were tested, retested and perfected. Thanks to the Bennettos and crew who have also done due diligence in eating a considerable amount of tiffin and have encouraged me along the way. Thanks to the many tasters and testers who have helped with fine-tuning the recipes so that they really work and that the end product looks like the one in the photographs.

Now I am known by my tiffin, wherever I go. I wish you well in your culinary adventures into tiffin and much happy tiffining in future.

Made in love,

Laura
xxx

54